Sweetbitter

Sundress Publications • Knoxville, TN

ISBN: 978-1-951979-28-7
Library of Congress: 2021950355
Published by Sundress Publications
www.sundresspublications.com

Editor: Erin Elizabeth Smith
Managing Editor: Anna Black
Editorial Assistant: Kanika Lawton
Editorial Interns: Stephi Cham, Katherine DeCoste, Ryleigh Wann

Colophon: This book is set in Bembo Std.

Cover Image: Kel Mur

Cover Design: Kristen Ton

Book Design: Erin Elizabeth Smith

Author Photo: Benjamin Aleshire

Sweetbitter

Stacey Balkun

Acknowledgements

Bear Review: "Lure"

Best New Poets 2018: "Wolf-Girl"

Burnt Offering (Porkbelly Publishing): "Two Girls on Fire" (reprint)

District Lit: "We Could Go Alone as Long as We Were Home Before Dark"

Fairy Tales and Folklore Re-Imagined (Between the Lines Publishing): "Desire is a Woman Selling a Basket of Fruit"

The Fourth River: "No Trespassing"

Grist: "What Weight"

Human/Kind: "Wilderness"

Iron Horse Literary Review: "Two Girls on Fire"

Menacing Hedge: "Possum Sapphic"

Plainsongs: "Once Upon a Time, There Were Two Girls"

Pleiades: "Two Truths and a Lie"

Rabbit Catastrophe: "Plants I Didn't Known Until After"

Talking Writing: "Element of Red"

Terrain.org: "The Water, the Truth, the Water," "In the Forest"

Wherewithal: sections of "The Book of Red" as "Mosquitos"

Zocalo Public Square: "No Book Would Tell Us Our Stories"

"Eulogy Ending in Red" was awarded First Place in the 2019 *Talking Writing* Poetry Contest.

"The Book of Red" was awarded Second Place in the 2018 Nan Snow Emerging Writer Awards.

"Two Girls on Fire" was a Finalist for the 2017 The Brittany Noakes Poetry Award and awarded Second Place in the 2017 *IHLR* Photo Finish Contest.

"The Water, the Truth, the Water" and "In the Forest" were awarded first place in the Tenth Annual *Terrain.org* Poetry Prize.

"The Water, the Truth, the Water" was a Finalist for the 2019 *Cream City* Poetry Award.

"Wolf-Girl" was awarded First Place in the 2017 William Faulkner Words of Wisdom Poetry Prize and was a semifinalist for the 2017 ProForma Prize from *Grist*.

Table of Contents

"As a sweet apple turns red on a high branch, high on the highest branch…"
—Sappho

"Cyanide in fruit seeds: how dangerous
is an apple?"
—*The Guardian*

The Possumtown neighborhood of Piscataway, NJ is home to a former Union Carbide plant, known to pollute the groundwater, and the former Middlesex Sampling Plant, a testing facility for the atomic bomb.

The Water, the Truth, the Water

Located fewer than 500 feet from the former site of the Wynnewood Swim Club in Piscataway, NJ is the chemical pond used by Union Carbide during the active phase of plant operation.

I go only as far as I dare
through the familiar neighborhood
behind the pool
collapsed razor wire squares the chemical pond
my shiver   my urge to wade in
to my insides   I can't rely on
or ask my dead
a thousand miles away
to see the diving board sticking out
the deep end   we count the steps
100 muddy paces between chlorine and acetone as
the stream
branches where I hang by

a full-grown possum-girl
past the NO TRESPASSING signs
a stream runs through and
it's 2018 and backhoes have torn at
the earth   scraped   the residue stuck
memory
the satellite maps   refresh
tomorrow I'll zoom close
pale tongue lapping
from swimming pool to waste pond
children   swam in both and
my body plunging to the bottom
the strength of my storyteller tail

the map

makes it seem farther

I want to know why
Nobody ever believed me

I keep scouring
but the water never recedes

I.

Once Upon a Time, There Were Two Girls

in the suburbs. One was a half-
girl and the other whole.

Through the woods,
they shimmered, telling stories

that sparkled like the radio,
like the oil-slicked creek.

      In the beginning,
               they said,

The crabapple birthed
a baby girl

      or

           The story goes
Lilith molded from the red

clay earth then Eve wrenched
from Adam's rib.

           They laughed
and they laughed. There,

no bear or blackberry,
just bramble. They believed

mothers plucked babies
from trees, wondered

if they'd ever want
for a man, even a kind one

cursed. How could there be
such thing as *happily*

                    ever after
when after all, all girls

have been swayed
by a forked tongue, held

captive as a crown?

Two Truths and a Lie

I.

We smoked because the boys did. We smoked Marlboro Reds. We'd light our Reds because the boys did, our Bics bright, sticking out the tight back pockets of our jeans because the boys liked to look and we liked to see the boys look because the boys did and because what could we have done to stop them? The way to the gas station was a path paved in our boys, in our smoke and compact mirrors. We swung plastic bags of candy bars because the boys did and because the boys did it, we let them kiss our open mouths, our lips tinted red as KitKat wrappers, as the *THANK YOU THANK YOU THANK YOU*, as the *OPEN* sign glowing in the Exxon's dark window.

II.

We were running. We were rundown. They ran us out of our woods

~

It was a test run. The river ran dry

~

What ran through our veins was never sap, syrup, sugar-sweet like

~

I ran my mouth, it runneth over. The boy who threatened still ran his hands across me even when

~

We ran out of cash, counted coins. Sometimes it was enough

~

We ran a six-minute mile but they could still do it in less. We raced, we flew, we
scrammed

~

We went running to our dads who threatened to pick a switch

III.

in the stillness that followed   our fathers pruned
and copsed   punished and grafted
us into   branch and bud
cambium   shunned and rooted
we had run and   the risk was
red   red
we rashed   ruin

A Forest (I)

The Cure

    into the dark

into the trees

the girl was
      running

     again and again and again

One Night in the Woods

A hundred hornets swarmed,
              a dress of buzz and sting, burnt cigarette

   in a can of soda. This was all we knew
       of wilderness. I thought I was Daphne,

          thought I was dead, drawing
             out the stingers in a stumbling haze.

          Apple-Child dissolved Benadryl
into a cup of Miracle-Gro and told me
       to drink. I wasn't sure I'd live, the poison coursing wild

               as the BCPs surging our stream. It cooled
          my honeyblood so I could almost breathe, a hum

    in my throat as I burrowed
        beneath a tree trunk, curled

and rooted—the taste a bitter
           linger, a new story salting my tongue.

In the Forest

we were storied, we were mud, rooted
into branch, Adam-less, pond scum, we were
not abandoned, not *boys hunt, girls sew* but river
otters and acorns, we were boar hunters run wild
with electric charge, riding crop, we were
riot, rushing past the dropped fruit
we could sing poorly but loud, tangled hair
and chalked lungs, we were baptized
above radioactive dirt, we were bicycle chains,
daisy chains, grass stains, more than crumbs
left for birds: mammalian, marsupial, we could swing
from high on the highest branch to crack the surface of the creek
we did not dream of escape until we did, each tree a girl
who couldn't scream, our bones ringing like bells

Why The Neighbors Told Us We Weren't Allowed to Talk to Boys

Because *they'd smell bad and be mean*

Because *they never would brush their ugly teeth*

Because *we've caught them with a heat-changing novelty lighter*
            painted with a pin-up girl, lingerie waning into skin as they held her

Because *the radio would say* give it up to me *and we'd all sing along*

Because *they'd beg and plead and we've always told you to know better*
            (so we knew better and only did what we wanted, when)

Because *they could play "Iron Man" on the keypad of the payphone in the park*
            (but we liked that)

Because *one boy sold coke in his treehouse and don't you remember*
            how his mother finally called the cops, on her own son

Because *another one, later, would burn his family's house down, accidentally,*
                        strung out on drugs

Because *then even Alan would drop out of school for a while*
                        and we all feared he'd turn up dead

Because *he didn't, he'd get his shit together instead but still*

Because *he would always be so much older than you, seventeen years cutting*
$\qquad\qquad\qquad\qquad\qquad\qquad\qquad$ *like a switchblade*

Because *if you're not careful, he'll soon coax you out of your dress in the back of a car*
$\qquad$ *parked in his grandmother's driveway* $\qquad$ (as if neither of us tore at his pants, eager)

Because *they rode dirt bikes into the woods, cleared a path along the chain link fence*

Because *another one would disappear, just one day be gone*
$\qquad\qquad\qquad$ *and another would hang himself*
$\qquad\qquad\qquad\qquad$ *using his own belt, his boy body dangled like a receiver*

Because *we don't like your friends, who will all be at the funeral, and so*
$\qquad\qquad\qquad\qquad\qquad$ *you're forbidden to go*

Because *you'd go anyway, all the time, shimmying out windows and down*
$\qquad\qquad\qquad\qquad$ *the gutters clung hollow against your girlish weight and*

Because *see—look at their bad influence. They did this to you, all of this* done
$\qquad\qquad\qquad\qquad$ *to you and still you should have known better,*
$\qquad\qquad\qquad\qquad\qquad$ *you hang-up, you broken slut, you girl*

Possum Sapphic

Not rodent, not girl, hands pink and soft as want.
For them, I sang this nocturne: another drink.
Crushed my empty-can heart into the trash bag,
dragged it to the curb.

Lure

Before the boys came   with Milwaukee's Best
the boys came   with bottle rockets
and before that   books of matches
they'd flare   tossed in our hair
just to hear us   screech
and before   the boys came with
Leathermans   the boys came
with sticks they'd use   to poke
at the backs of our knees   at our thighs and once
we went   fishing together, popcorn
tied to a shoelace   we'd take turns
dragged through the creek   they swore it
every bite   all was theirs
reeled in   fighting
for breath   through the shallows
                              even then

of course we knew

who was the hunter
who was the prey

What Weight

is a thimble,
a spinning needle?

A cough of apple
flesh caught in a throat?

A poisoned splinter
shoved under a nail?

A glass coffin?
A stepmother's swollen

jaw? The pucker
of a newborn's lips

suckling? Panties,
torn or pulled

or stored
in an evidence locker?

The air that makes up
most of a chain link fence?

An emptied make-up clutch
or a smudge

of eyeshadow?
The shadow of a man

where there was no man?
The furrow

in parted hair
where once there was

a crown?
The first bird call

after? The blonde hairs
on her arms pinned

against peat moss?
A palate of asbestos

and the trail it sifts?
Insects and microbes

chewing pine needle,
apple core, any thin rush

of blood and turning it
into dirt from which grows

the forest, the red–leafed
clover, the white-tailed

deer; feeding that
which feeds the wolf?

Half-Sapphic with the Smell of Fear

We knew never to
step upon the skunk cabbage
so its scent meant someone
else. Close.

Possum Kingdom
Toadies

             tonight

  a   man

      the
         dark

a lie

   with hair
  and skin

Wolf-Girl

I read the stories

I snarled

tangled hair

his papa's gun

sweet as honey wine

as grandmother

in a game of rummy

face down

I tell him

I beg him closer

I prowl around the edge of

blossom: both will wither

I could howl

I want him

I sharpen my teeth

I wore a tight red dress

into the woods

neighbor boy unholstering

said he wanted   a wolf

in a picnic basket

worrying her cards

the queens all frown

leave the gun

where you can't reach

he will show me what men want

shame   rose, apple

unless I take him first

if I tried

gone

II.

The Book of Red

It was not a sunny day. I knew
not to stray far, but I didn't

know why. My grandmother lived at the edge
of the trees, across from the public pool

set into the woods, oaks spreading
almost all the way to River Road to meet

a barbed wire fence set
around the old Union Carbide-Bakelite factory.

I've tried to read the story
but it keeps changing and now

the land has sold. A superfund site
on one side of my woods

and a brownfield on the other: more
and more dads got sick but I knew

not to question, not to wander
past the red lawn flags unfurling in the dirt.

~

When Little Red Cap entered the woods
a wolf came up to her. She

    did not know what   wicked   was.

The wolf thought   "Now that sweet
young thing is a tasty bite for me"

~

There was never the taste of a hunter
or a woodsman. There was only a dog,
off leash, a chase through the woods

into my grandmother's garage.
I slammed the laundry room door
just in time or maybe

it was a dream. The neighbor boy
had three mastiffs, wild things
that would jump the fence and chase girls

on their way to school and in August
they came for me. I can still smell the chemical
scent of fabric softener, the stale air

in that small room, my back against
the door, legs shocked from running, a barb
linked in my chest. If the dog had a name

like *Suburbia*, I don't remember the collar
glinted against his neck.

~

In   this suburban town, behind
a chain link fence topped by barbed wire   is
*   a   monument to the atomic age: a three-acre*
mound of radioactive dirt   .

The dirt   is   the Middlesex Sampling Plant,
one of several top-secret sites where
uranium was tested
*   which built the atomic bomb.*

*   the Environmental Protection Agency*
would add the site to the Superfund list

*   But residents of this community   are numb.*
there was   some   radioactivity

*   and*
*   ground water contamination.*

*   awareness of the site   came   1960,*
accidentally   Geiger counters were stunned

~

Geigered murky with dirt and chlorine,
it was never warm, even in August,
never full. Never mirror.

All empty lounge chairs marking
red stripes on our thighs, the only
two girls sitting poolside. Never

the way me and the girls dreamed it:
just a gush from a green hose
a glance from a lifeguard

busy skimming the glint surface
of the deep end, its cracked
plaster bottom we practiced

reaching: pumping our legs.
Our breaths held stitched.

~

Everything itched:
sunburn, poison ivy, and when

we walked to the pool,
chlorine burned our eyes, stung

our scrapes, old scars pink as apples
on our thighs. It was almost the new

millennium. We crossed our arms
over cramping bellies, afraid

the boys could smell our blood
or see the bulge of tampons

awkward in our pockets. They threw
apples across our paths

but we didn't stop to look.
We itched where the hair grew

under our armpits, two girls
sweet as fruit—we never smiled

with our fluoride-paled teeth.

~

One   chemical pond is in the woods
of Piscataway, New Jersey
                              used by Union Carbide
Its main purpose:

Hazardous and exotic chemicals
would   drain
to the pond and later
           pump back

to   be distilled
              to remove acetone
and other hazardous chemicals.
      This process was overall

                    harmful to the environment
                         and polluted the groundwater.

~

41

We waded in the clear ground-stream,
mosquito arms

bramble-nourished, red
as the nicks that would welt up

when we learned
to shave. We scratched skin

raw, aware
of our chests

poked against
our tee shirts, and when

we heard the boys howl,
we made ourselves

small. Trespassers,
still as trees.

~

Radioactivity Assessment: *Recreational Trespasser:*

This receptor represents land use by a trespassing adolescent

(age 6 to 15 years) living in a nearby residential area.

This receptor is designed to account for occasional exposure to contaminated media

during recreational activities such as hiking and biking, for two hours per week

~

Rewritten, recreated, weak, we couldn't account
for how the story would go

>   *they kept telling us*
>   *that there was no health danger*

new houses kept going up, and then
the neighborhood pool. It was all

>   *deemed clean*
>   *by the standards of the time*

>   *But then these guys in white protective suits*
>   *started doing all this digging and testing*

in the early 80s, just before
we were born, just before we arrived red-faced

from racing to the pool, daring each other
to cross the railroad trestle

>   *By 1997, 24 of the 46 sites*
>   *had been cleaned. the cleanups   not   completed*

over Possumtown Road. We'd come home
soaking wet after swearing never to swim

>   *until 2006 at the earliest*

in the brook or the pond

After all, we always promised

       we'd pay attention.

~

All that attention, and still
I didn't see his teeth and still

it's my fault I didn't see his teeth
even when he smiled

and took my hand. Other girls
were going. He had grabbed
a girl's ass on the school bus

and we all chose
to forget. His mom

had just died,
it seemed like he needed
me. I wanted to go

with him, and then
I didn't. When I wouldn't

take off my bikini, he grew
impatient. Said I should
let him

untie the straps or
I should leave.

He reached up
and I didn't resist.
My bathing suit

was red. I was scarcely a girl
in a body unfinished.

~

The wolf had scarcely finished

      when he jumped from the bed

with a single leap   "Where are you going
                        Little Red Cap?"

"To grandmother's"   And she ran off

      going further
     and further into the woods

~

We wanted to wander further for wild berries
and a swim in the creek. We wanted
a life like the storybooks, all song
birds and happily ever, not this

barbed wire and chain link. Not
chlorine-stained hair, unwrapping bomb
pops from the ice cream truck.
The offices knew the health effects

would not surface for up to 50 years,
a 1967 Union Carbide memo proved: "make hay
while the sun shines." It's overcast. It's shady
except in winter when the oaks cough up clumps

of rusted leaves and we can see almost
all the way to the factory from just behind the pool.

~

The   is a good quarter hour
from here in the woods, under
the three large oak trees.

You must know the place.

~

You must know the place
where Little Red Cap entered the woods.
There was supposed to be a hunter
in this suburban town, somewhere

in the murk. The dirt, the chlorine:
everything always smelled and we itched.
A chemical pond at the edge of our woods,
we waded in, waiting

to be rewritten, recreated. Weak,
I couldn't account for the forest
or the trees, paying too much attention to
the wolf we always wanted

to find and cut open. No berries. No choice.
It was not a sunny day.

III.

Element of Red

We burned through September, rusted
oaks and maples refusing to give up
their brilliance. In the heat of late afternoon,

the factory blew its snowy dissonance through
our woods: chemical smell of popcorn and dryer sheets.

She was Apple-Child and I was a fistful of clover
until I got a splinter from her swing set
and she ran away screaming, terrified of AIDS

because by second grade, they'd taught us to fear
each other. I skipped church

to climb trees, a possum-girl, and none of us knew
about the radiation or groundwater
or how the rectory was built

above contaminated fill. If we could leave it all
behind, simply step into a painting, we may not

choose *Arcadia.* We could be capable of anything
or maybe just tumored, paranoid. *Well, if you have
lost your mind, blame Union Carbide.*

Blame the Atomic Bomb, Alan tells me,
it's not my fault. We were all baptized

in radioactive dirt. Given bread and told
to stay away from blood. As far as I know,
the river never caught fire. But

our throats itch, rough enough to strike a match.

A Forest (II)

The Cure

Come closer

        girl

    follow
    follow

      my
        voice

       it's too late

No Books Would Tell Us Our Stories

Apple-Child and I once hovered in my driveway,
hopscotching between maple seeds
helicoptered to the asphalt that shines

near-molten in the August sun.
In that moment we wanted
this leap to never land, levitating

above the flat front yard, grass seeded
green each spring, my dad pushing
the Miracle Grow sprayer up

and down up and down the lawn
so the clover would yellow and fall.
Never a skinned knee or burning

elbow to kiss. Never lips to press
together. No grandmother's or neighbors'
or father's funerals to attend. No.

In the hot air in which we floated,
there was no future, no high school,
no tumor lodged like an acorn

in my father's neck, obstructing the nerves
like the piles of twigs we dammed
in the creek to block the cold rush

and no EPA or Army Corps of Engineers
to study the contamination levels
in our water, fifteen years later. No,

just sun lifting the humid curtain
between excitement and pain, tale
and hard truth—it will be years

before we understand
what *occasional exposure* can do
to a lung or spinal cord,

taut in that space before we hit
the pavement, bare feet unburned
from years of hard callous.

We tossed a peach pit across chalk lines,
committed only to each other, to the bare bones
of summer chirping by as slowly as our limbs

unlengthened, not yet feeling trapped
in a *before* or *after*, the air stilled and time
just a caterpillar crawling across my wrist.

We Could Go Alone as Long
as We Were Home Before Dark

For Halloween, I decide I'm Daphne
but everyone thinks I'm a tree
since Apple-Child is Eve, though it's so cold
she must wear a sweater over her leaves.

The twigs in her hair seem accidental,
like she had tumbled into me. We trick-or-treat
by the river, then at the new development
edging Union Carbide land, fenced off

from the condos where we can ring
two doorbells at once. My root-legs move slow.
She crunches dry leaves underfoot.
A neighbor gives us each a candied apple

and I hold mine to my lips, deciding
to lick or bite. It's the most delicious thing.

Being the Girl Not the Princess

Being the girl not the princess means	rags, or
Being the girl not the princess means	riches, but then
Being the girl not the princess means	you're selfish, awful as an unweeded garden
Being the girl not the princess means	no ladybug would land on your knee
Being the girl not the princess means	crawling to more poverty or certain death
Being the girl not the princess means	you've done something wrong
Being the girl not the princess means	men will start to watch or toss gold
Being the girl not the princess means	apples across your path
Being the girl not the princess means	no one will tell you how
Being the girl not the princess means	you're never safe and
Being the girl not the princess means	wasps will chase and sting and
Being the girl not the princess means	you will never forget that blushing hurt, that
Being the girl not the princess means	*acceptable risk*, though
Being the girl not the princess means	you will always be punished for

Desire is Blackberries

Apple-Child and I
      picked blackberries
            in the field behind the pool,

filling a plastic pumpkin
      from Halloween.
            We licked each other's

pricked fingers,
      juice and blood
            together. We met

when we were seven,
      swore to be sisters
            all our lives but sometimes

I still hate her,
      even tangled
            in honeysuckle

and poison ivy.
      We tried to learn
            what sweetness was.

            What hurt.

Two Girls on Fire

blazed through the forest, Bics tight
in closed fists, painted lips

smoking. Their tongues lit up
like oak leaves, bronzed as books

of matches tucked into back pockets,
their story and its ending yet

unwritten. This, their last summer
together, every day above 90

and the old crab apple trunk split
down the center, sap

dripping through the heat
of another drought, thick

as the blood that stained
their shorts, turning snapped twigs

into kindling, rough as the shadows
around the mouths of boys

who edged against the tree line,
boys smelling of pitch

and butane, boys spilling whiskey
onto the fire, eager and aching for flame.

Apple-Child Went to Homecoming

and I went to a house party
instead. I sipped from a glass bottle
of beer, ate a heel of crusty bread
or was it pretzels? The radio said, *feed*

your head, so I practiced cartwheels
on the tallest boy's yellowed lawn, a tangle
of garden and sparks.
I wanted to trust him

though I knew better.
When he took me
to watch the high school fireworks
from a drainage pit

near the high school,
time stopped. I tripped
in a rabbit hole, fence-hopping
and wading through tall weeds

to the mouth of a concrete tube
yawned so wide we could sit side-
by-side, far from the familiar,
sulfur stench. Every echo

resounded through us,
gunpowder glint above,

the drought so bad we feared
all the grass would burst

into flame. It was just the way
the story book said: the more
I flailed the further I fell.
My instincts conflicted:

to run or play dumb,
dead. It was how gently he asked
that made me resist. The hair
on his knuckles that lured me in.

2002

This is the year the old crabapple yields more
than a single fruit. The year no one mows the dandelion field

across from the public pool. This is the year we learn
what it's like to stop trying. The year we'll walk home
from school and find a field knee-deep in clover.
The year Apple-Child will lie in it and disappear

from sight and I won't panic. The year we'll drown
in the green, dirt under our nails. A neighbor boy will find us

curious, and we won't be afraid. The year we'll remember
the winter when we walked the salted street, street plows

piling the sidewalks high. An older boy from school would turn
the corner in his truck, see us trapped between the cold puddles
and a drift. We'd hear him hit the gas and know
for the first time, there was nothing we could do.

This is the year we'll keep rocks in our coat pockets.

The year Apple-Child will unwrap a Plan B
and we'll hold hands, feeling odd at our lack
of remorse. This is the year our lighters will burn hot
and be lost, the year of vodka poured into cups

of clean snow. Year of thirst, of throats and tongues
burning with what we want. What we want finally

said by more than gesture. Year we don't grasp for lightning
bugs the first warm night in June. Year of dark
lipstick and yellow teeth, more snarl, less smile
every time we're asked. This is the year

we'll learn not to swallow
back each moment but to take a hard bite, to chew it slow.

Rotten Apples
The Smashing Pumpkins

Dirty

        love

I go

    to

The other side of

    longing

Restless

     in
   the dirt

We Couldn't Know What Wasn't Poison

Apple-Child and I hunted
for mushrooms after the storm.
The downed oaks made good homes
for everything we feared
to eat. Wet ground gave way
to a spring beneath our feet
so we cupped our palms
and drank the cool, clear water
from each other's hands and there,
tangled in a steeple of golden
limbs and benedictions, my body
became her wine. Everything was wet
and soft, the knotted bun of her
dark hair falling loose.

               When we saw
the first chanterelle, we nudged it
with a twig: how tender it gave way,
opening to our cautious touch
and golden. The stories never said.

We pretended nothing happened.
The water ran muddy long after the rain.

Sapphic for the Inside of Her Mouth

the redbuds burst swollen
as entrails. We dug in
with our thumbnails,
parted sepal from petal
and they fell, one
by one, onto each
of our pink tongues.

She Tells Me the River is a Monster

Because it continues to cut away the land
without pulling her house any closer
to mine.

Wilderness

Sleater-Kinney

           on the way
                back

     desire
     split   in half

Plants I Didn't Know Until After

Sycamore and sweetgum gifting their spiky pods.
Blue hydrangeas blooming like moons.
Turkey fig, delicious waddle and spread of each huge leaf.
Cypress with its elbows and knees gasping for air.
Joshua tree propheting along the side of the highway.
Bird of paradise and its violent beaks.
Juniper berries before they're crushed into gin.
Apple-pear bearing fruit that's both and neither.
Loquat which I still don't understand.
White peach and the pit's bloody center.
Blood orange with its red juice running.
Star jasmine trying to smudge the night clean.
Kumquat and the crunch of rind under dull teeth,
how wicked it feels to eat each orange whole.

Orchard Sapphic

High, on the highest branch where no one but me
could reach, Apple-Child hid, pink skin a flash
through the burnt red leaves—for a time she was mine.
Never completely.

Aubade for Lying Fallow

what else is left
to say
            about the grass?

a body is a body

a field, unpartitioned

a field is not two curtains
meeting, draped in soft overlap

and I am holding
                        my composure

a drawstring

                waiting waiting
                for your touch

we are all meant to be parted
the grass too was meant to be parted

I am learning   how to open
you   are walking away

Conservation Effort

a cento

Night covers the pond with its wing.
No place to go now but into deep ground.

Absences allow us one power over them:
you have to imagine a shadow hill hiding inside.

The water is a mess.
The world is blue at its edges and in its depths.

The water seems suspended,
the geese flying low over the marsh.

We say of them what we want,
reaching out for the unlimited.

Even now this landscape is assembling:
it's truth against truth.

Sometimes we miss the things we have lost,
even if we love the water we swim in now.

No Trespassing

There was such a thing once
as a cello. As an apple
we could eat, two girls alone

in the orchard long abandoned.
We crouched on our knees,
unearthed pale mushrooms,

delicate as mythology, as the deer
we used to see bounding.
There was such a thing

once as music and we made it
up, our lips chapped
from whistling through the ragged

weeds soured by the plant
that used to grow here, all tall
walls and atoms split and once

there was such a thing as power
but we were never the ones
who held it, wild in the woods

with our voices and our stories
and our bow-less hands. We held
each other, tied shoelaces to fallen limbs,

two Atalantas, golden and strong
for our make-believe hunts—fingertips
burning, thighs burning, tongues burnt

already. We didn't know what to chase
so we became the prize, appraised
and bound together, our girl bodies

moving always in silence.
We never were taught how to sing.

Desire is a Woman Selling a Basket of Fruit

Nobody ever told me I was beautiful
not even at the artist residency
when I was the only woman

among seven men, so deep
in the woods, I got lost

in the old stories. Once upon
a time, there was a hometown,
a best friend, half–

imagined. We did our best
to grow up, took the chance

when we could
and fled but then I kept
to myself, a box of red wine

on my bookshelf, left
the French doors wide open to let in

the breeze—I made it easy
for a wolf or witch to find me
but isn't that what you think

to do when you know
of nothing else—choose

the glossiest fruit?
I always reach for the apple
to remember her,

a small girl reckless
as razor blades or a poisoned

ruby set in a broken crown.
I always wish the seeds
to be what burns.

Timeline, "From the Book of Red"

1943   Middlesex Sampling Plant began to sample ores.

1945   Union Carbide's Bound Brook plant began to expose individuals to asbestos until 1980.

1948   A contractor dumps dirt from the Middlesex site at a municipal landfill; this dirt is used as "clean fill" and goes out to building projects, including Our Lady of Mount Virgin Church.

1955   The Atomic Energy Commission took over the Middlesex site and used it for limited sampling of thorium-bearing ores, until 1967.

1960   Geiger counters register radiation at the Middlesex site.

1964   Wynnewood Swim Club opens on the same block as the Union Carbide chemical pool (approximate date; as of 2018, the club claims to be operating for "over fifty years").

1967   The buildings and grounds of the Middlesex Sampling Plant were decontaminated. It was deemed clean "by the standards of the time" and the company moved on.

1967   Union Carbide publishes an internal memo that proved the company knew asbestos exposure caused cancer.

1980s   Middlesex Borough hires its own consultants to get an independent opinion on the dangers of radiation.

1997   Across the US, only 24 of the 48 sites formerly used for nuclear projects have yet been cleaned.

2000   Department of Energy's original projected completion date of cleanup for the Middlesex site.

2006   The US Army Corps of Engineers' revised projected completion date of cleanup for the Middlesex site.

2017   Lincoln Equities Group LLC and its partner Real Capital Solutions sell the 228-acre industrial property, which formerly housed a former plastics manufacturing plant and was later remediated by Union Carbide Corp, to the Rockefeller Group for $57 million.

2020   Former site of the Wynnewood Swim Club now deemed a Regulated Wetland Transition Area Adjacent to Freshwater Wetlands and access is restricted. The pool has been filled in.

Notes

"The Book of Red" contains text taken from "Little Red Cap" by the Brothers Grimm; "Three-Acre Legacy of the Atom Bomb: A Pile of Radioactive Dirt Awaits Cleanup in New Jersey," *The New York Times*, 1998, by Ronald Smother; "Chemical Pond" Wikipedia entry; "Soils Operable Unit Record of Decision: Middlesex Sampling Plant," prepared by the US Army Corps of Engineers, 2005; and "Union Carbide" entry from The Mesothelioma Center, 2018, by Matt Mauney.

"Conservation Effort" contains lines from Elizabeth Bishop's "At the Fishouses," Louise Gluck's *The House on Marshland,* Sarah Broome's *The Yellow House*, Rebecca Solnit's *A Field Guide to Getting Lost*, Kate Chopin's *The Awakening*, Robert Sullivan's *The Meadowlands*, Steve Mentz's *Ocean*, Sleater-Kinney's "Wilderness," and Atlas Obscura's entry on the Meadowlands.

"Cyanide in fruit seeds: how dangerous is an apple?" appeared in *The Guardian* on October 11, 2015.

"A Forest" is an erasure of lyrics © Fiction Songs Ltd., from songwriters Laurence Andrew Tolhurst, Robert James Smith, Simon Gallup, and Matthieu A. Harley.

"In the Forest" would not exist without Vievee Francis's "Back on the Ridge."

"It was Halloween or a Summer Day" would not exist without Catherine Pierce's "The Delinquent Girls."

"No Books Would Tell Us These Stories" would not exist without Nandini Dhar's "No History Books Would Tell Us Our Stories."

Thank You

Writing is not a solitary act. Much gratitude to everyone who encouraged each line of this book, especially Jenn Givhan, Clare Harmon, Kim Kotel, Aurelea River, and Erin Elizabeth Smith. Thank you to Thomas Centolella and Dorianne Laux for encouraging these poems to get weird in the desert. Thank you to Camille Dungy and Neil Aitken for seeing strength in these poems early on.

I offer the sincerest gratitude to the following fellowship programs for their support in researching and writing this book: Longleaf Writers Conference, Sundress Academy for the Arts, Taos Poetry Retreat, Taos Writers Conference, University of Mississippi Department of Graduate Studies, and The Wurlitzer Foundation.

About the Author

Stacey Balkun is the author of *Sweetbitter* and co-editor of *Fiolet & Wing: An Anthology of Domestic Fabulist Poetry*. Winner of the 2019 New South Writing Contest as well as Terrain.org's 10th Annual Contest, her work has appeared in *Best New Poets 2018, Mississippi Review, The Rumpus*, and several other anthologies and journals. Balkun holds an MFA from Fresno State and teaches creative writing online at The Poetry Barn and The Loft. Visit her online at www.staceybalkun.com.

Other Sundress Titles

Mouths of Garden
Barbara Fant
$16

Slaughter the One Bird
Kimberly Ann Priest
$16

The Valley
Esteban Rodriguez
$16

To Everything There Is
Donna Vorreyer
$16

nightsong
Ever Jones
$16

JAW
Albert Abonado
$16

Something Dark to Shine In
Inés Pujos
$16

Dad Jokes from Late in the Patriarchy
Amorak Huey
$16

What Nothing
Anna Meister
$16

Hood Criatura
féi hernandez
$16

Maps of Injury
Chera Hammons
$16

Lessons in Breathing Underwater
HK Hummel
$16

CPSIA information can be obtained
at www.ICGtesting.com
Printed in the USA
BVHW052055220222
629773BV00005B/238